Happy Mother's Day

THE NIGHT BEFORE
BEFORE
MOTHER'S
DAY

To our mothers

Doug MacLeod & Judy Horacek

THE NIGHT BEFORE MOTHER'S DAY

Andrews McMeel
Publishing, LLC

Kansas City • Sydney • London

First published in 2012 by Allen & Unwin, Australia

Andrews McMeel Publishing, LLC
an Andrews McMeel Universal company
1130 Walnut Street, Kansas City, Missouri 64106

www.andrewsmcmeel.com

ISBN 978-1-4494-2228-8

12 13 14 15 16 TEN 10 9 8 7 6 5 4 3 2 1

ATTENTION: SCHOOLS AND BUSINESSES
Andrews McMeel books are available at quantity discounts
with bulk purchase for educational, business, or sales
promotional use. For information, please e-mail the
Andrews McMeel Publishing Special Sales Department:
specialsales@amuniversal.com

'Twas the night
before Mother's Day—
Mom lay awake.
The sense of excitement
Was too much to take.

She knew that tomorrow
Would bring her such joys
As gifts from her daughter
And two darling boys.

Her little girl, Courtney,
Would brighten her day
By giving her something
She'd made out of clay.

A pottery teacup
From art class at school,
And Mom would say, "Lovely!"
Since honesty's cruel.

"I simply adore it,
My clever young daughter,
And why should I care
That it doesn't hold water?"

And what of son David
And dear little Paul?
They'd buy her some soap
From the Mother's Day stall.

Some lavender powder
And bath salts, as well,
And other such items
For people who smell.

They'd pull up some flowers
To hand her with pride,
Forgetting the puddle
They'd stepped in outside.

And neither would notice
The footprints they'd made
In all of the places
Where carpet was laid.

They'd give her some chocolates,
The ones she liked best,
And Mom would eat two
While the kids ate the rest.

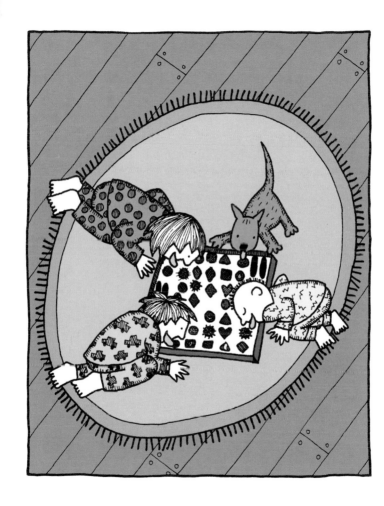

She'd open her card,
And the children would titter
As Mom ended up
With a bed full of glitter.

And Mom kept on thinking
(The clock had struck three).
She thought of the morning—
What fun it would be...

She'd stay in her bedroom
And not be concerned
By cries from the kitchen
As breakfast was burned.

The kids would leave dishes
And a mess on the shelf.
(They knew that a kitchen
Got cleaned by itself.)

They'd bring Mom her breakfast.
She'd tell them, "Well done!"
And Dad would look happy,
Though he would eat none.

She'd kiss them and thank them,
Her three little pets,
Then munch on the muffins
That looked like briquettes.

And just when she'd struggle
To eat any more,
They'd feed her the omelet
They'd dropped on the floor.

When breakfast was over,
They'd all go away,
So Mom could relax
For the rest of the day.

She'd sit in her armchair
With nothing to do
But rest from ten-thirty
Till ten-thirty-two.

And Mom kept on thinking.
(The clock had struck four).
She thought of the evening
And what was in store...

The children would wander,
Then home they would come
With something especially
Borrowed for Mom.

A DVD movie
To show their devotion,
Concerning a vampire
Who kills in slow motion.

And Dad would say, "Sweetheart,
This day is your own.
I'll organize dinner.
Just hand me the phone."

He'd order a pizza
With pineapple rings,
And Mom would remove them
(She hated the things).

Then Paul would say, "Mommy,
It's all right for you,
But why don't we celebrate
Children's Day, too?"

Both Courtney and David
Would sulk in despair,
And Mom would agree
It was grossly unfair.

But during the movie
A thought would occur—
She'd wish that the vampire
Were actually her.

She'd think about Courtney
And David and Paul,
And how she'd take pleasure
In biting them all.

And as for their father,
Who sat drinking beer,
To snap off his head
Seemed a lovely idea.

Disturbed by the notion,
She'd call her own mother.
And kindly and gently
They'd comfort each other.

"You've had a hard day, dear?"
Her mother would guess,
"Of handcrafted presents?
And mayhem? And mess?

"Well, come around later,
Let's both drink some tea—
From leaky clay teacups
You once gave to me."

Then Mom stopped her thinking.
The silence was deep.
She sighed, then she chuckled,
And fell sound asleep.